LOWERCASE CURSIVE ALPHABET

Practice tracing the lowercase alphabet until you are comfortable with each one. Remember that you can trace over each letter more than once.

A B C D E F G H I J K L M N O P Q R S T U V W Y X Z

a   *b*   *c*   *d*

e   *f*   *g*   *h*

i   *j*   *k*   *l*

m   *n*   *o*   *p*

q   *r*   *s*   *t*

u   *v*   *w*   *x*

y   *z*

Are you ready to learn how to write numbers in cursive? For each exercise, trace and follow the numbered arrows, practice following the dot-to-dot letters, and then complete the independent practice. **Ready? Set. Go!**

One   one   **1**

One

one

Two   two   

Two

two

Three   three   

Three

three

Four   four   4

Four

four

Five   five   5

Five

five

Six   six   6

Six

six

Seven   seven   7

Seven

seven

Eight   eight   8

Eight

eight

Nine   nine   9

Nine

nine

Ten   *ten*   **10**

Ten

ten

Eleven eleven   **11**

Eleven

eleven

Twelve twelve   **12**

Twelve

twelve

Thirteen thirteen 13

Thirteen

thirteen

Fourteen fourteen 14

Fourteen

fourteen

Fifteen fifteen 15

Fifteen

fifteen

Awesome Job!

Are you ready to learn how to write colors in cursive? For each exercise, trace and follow the numbered arrows, practice following the dot-to-dot letters and then complete the independent practice. Ready? Set. Go!

Red   red

Red

red

Blue   blue

Blue

blue

Yellow   yellow

Yellow

yellow

Green green

Green

green

Purple purple

Purple

purple

Orange orange

Orange

orange

Violet violet

Violet

violet

Pink pink

Pink

pink

Brown brown

Brown

brown

Black

Black   Black

Teal

Teal   Teal

Gold

Gold   Gold

Well done!

Are you ready to learn how to write the seasons and the months of the year in cursive? For each exercise, trace and follow the numbered arrows, practice following the dot-to-dot letters, use the blank areas for independent practice. Ready? Set. Go!

Winter

winter

Winter

winter

Spring

spring

Spring

spring

Summer

summer

Summer

summer

Fall

fall

Fall

fall

January

January   January

February

February   February

March

March   March

April

April   April

May

May   May

June

June   June

July

July   July

August

August   August

September

September   September

October

October   October

November

November   November

December

December   December

That was fun?

Are you ready to learn how to write your name and other first names in cursive? Begin by printing your first and last name on the line below and then write your name in cursive on the practice lines below. Ready? Set. Go!

First Name

Last Name

Here are several first names. Practice writing each one in cursive.

Emma

Emma   Emma

Ava

Ava   Ava

Zoey

Zoey   Zoey

Aiden

Aiden   Aiden

Roger

Roger   Roger

Noah

Noah   Noah

Ethan

Ethan   Ethan

OTHER BOOKS IN THE SERIES

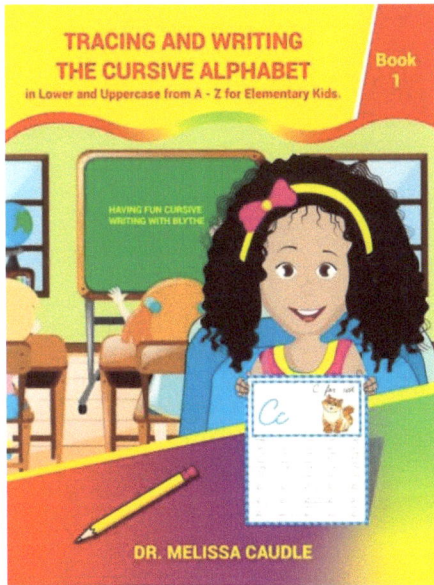

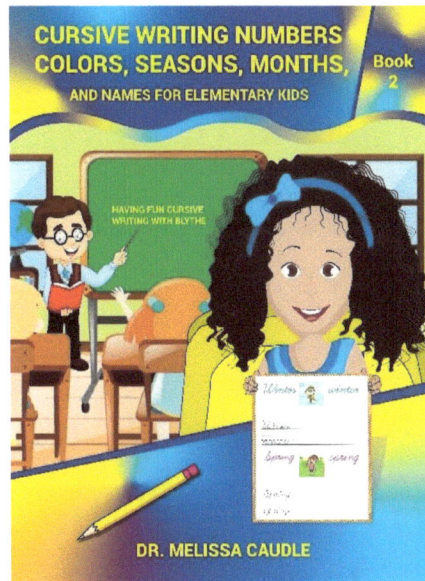

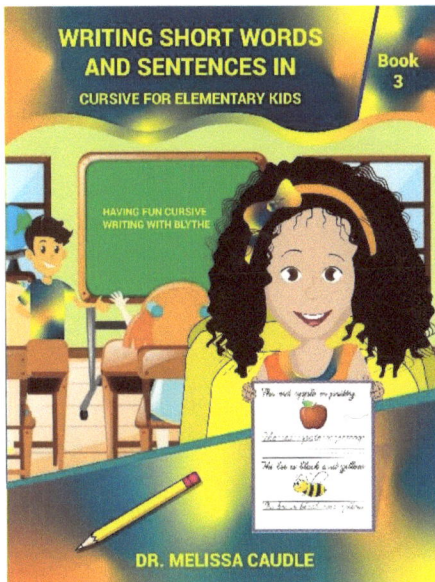

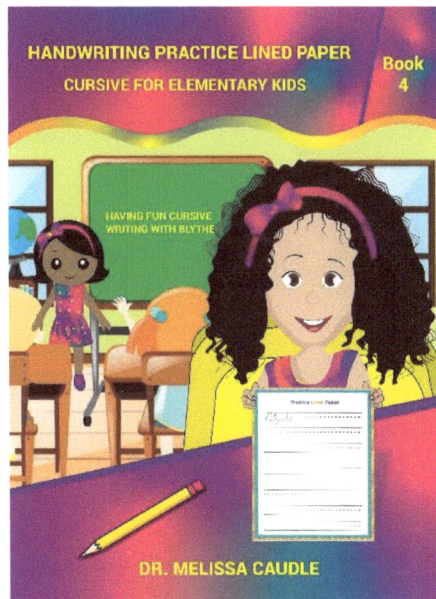

**TRACING AND WRITING
THE CURSIVE ALPHABET**
in Lower and Uppercase from A - Z for Elementary Kids.

Book 1

HAVING FUN CURSIVE
WRITING WITH BLYTHE

DR. MELISSA CAUDLE

**CURSIVE WRITING NUMBERS
COLORS, SEASONS, MONTHS,**
AND NAMES FOR ELEMENTARY KIDS

Book 2

HAVING FUN CURSIVE
WRITING WITH BLYTHE

DR. MELISSA CAUDLE

**WRITING SHORT WORDS
AND SENTENCES IN**
CURSIVE FOR ELEMENTARY KIDS

Book 3

HAVING FUN CURSIVE
WRITING WITH BLYTHE

DR. MELISSA CAUDLE

HANDWRITING PRACTICE LINED PAPER
CURSIVE FOR ELEMENTARY KIDS

Book 4

HAVING FUN CURSIVE
WRITING WITH BLYTHE

DR. MELISSA CAUDLE

AVAILABLE ON AMAZON

Cursive Beginning

HANDWRITING

WORKBOOK

FOR 2nd – 6th Grade

The Big Coloring Book to Learn Upper and Lowercase Cursive Writing that Includes the Alphabet, Seasons, Months, Numbers, Names, Short Words, & Sentences

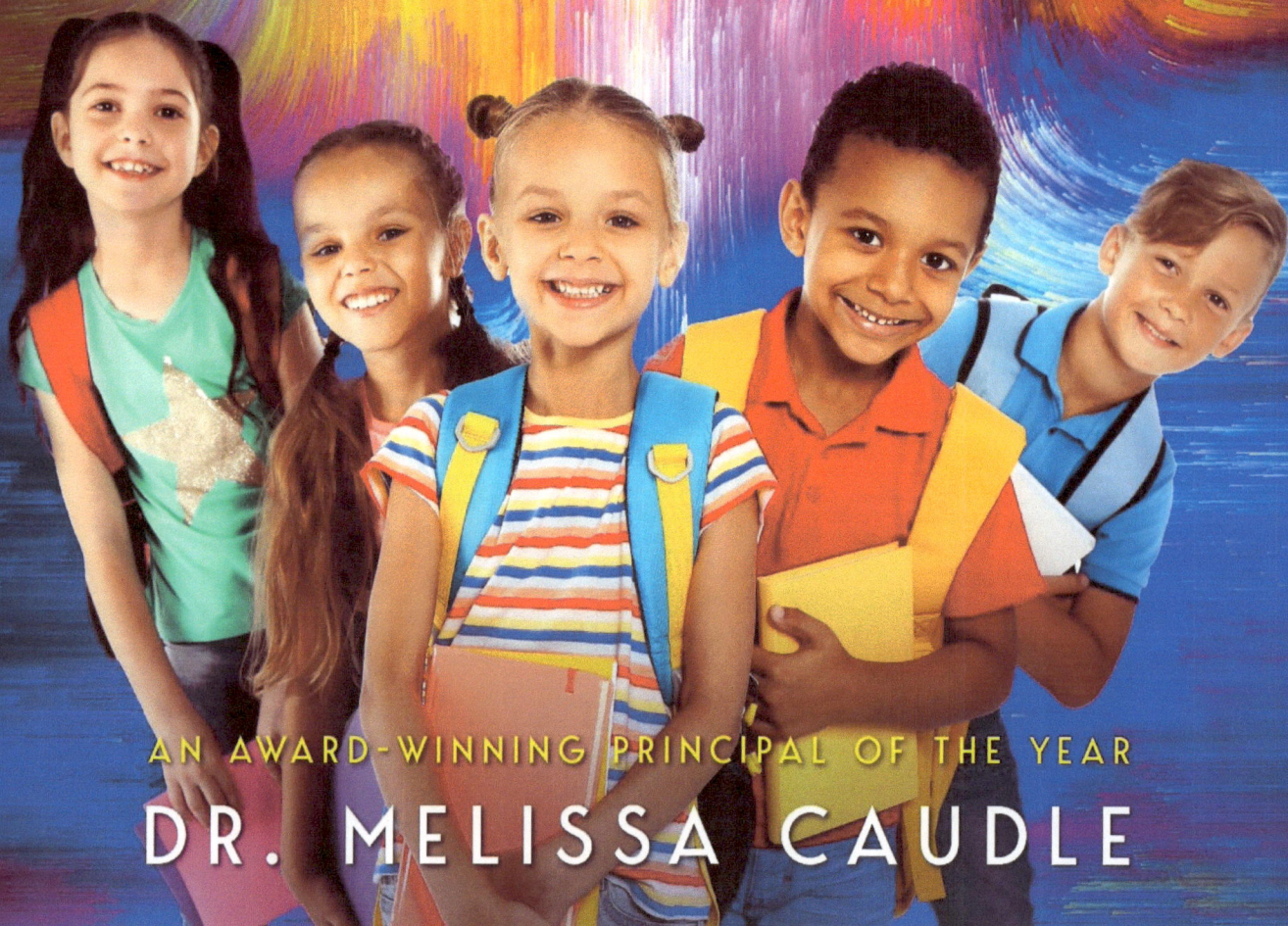

AN AWARD-WINNING PRINCIPAL OF THE YEAR

DR. MELISSA CAUDLE

THE **AMAZINGLY** *Fun Jumbo Activity*

BOOK FOR KIDS

Crossword Puzzles, Mazes, Color by Numbers, Wordsearch, Spot the Difference, Tracing, Unscramble the Words, Connect the Dots, Identify Shapes, Matching, and More Fun Stuff

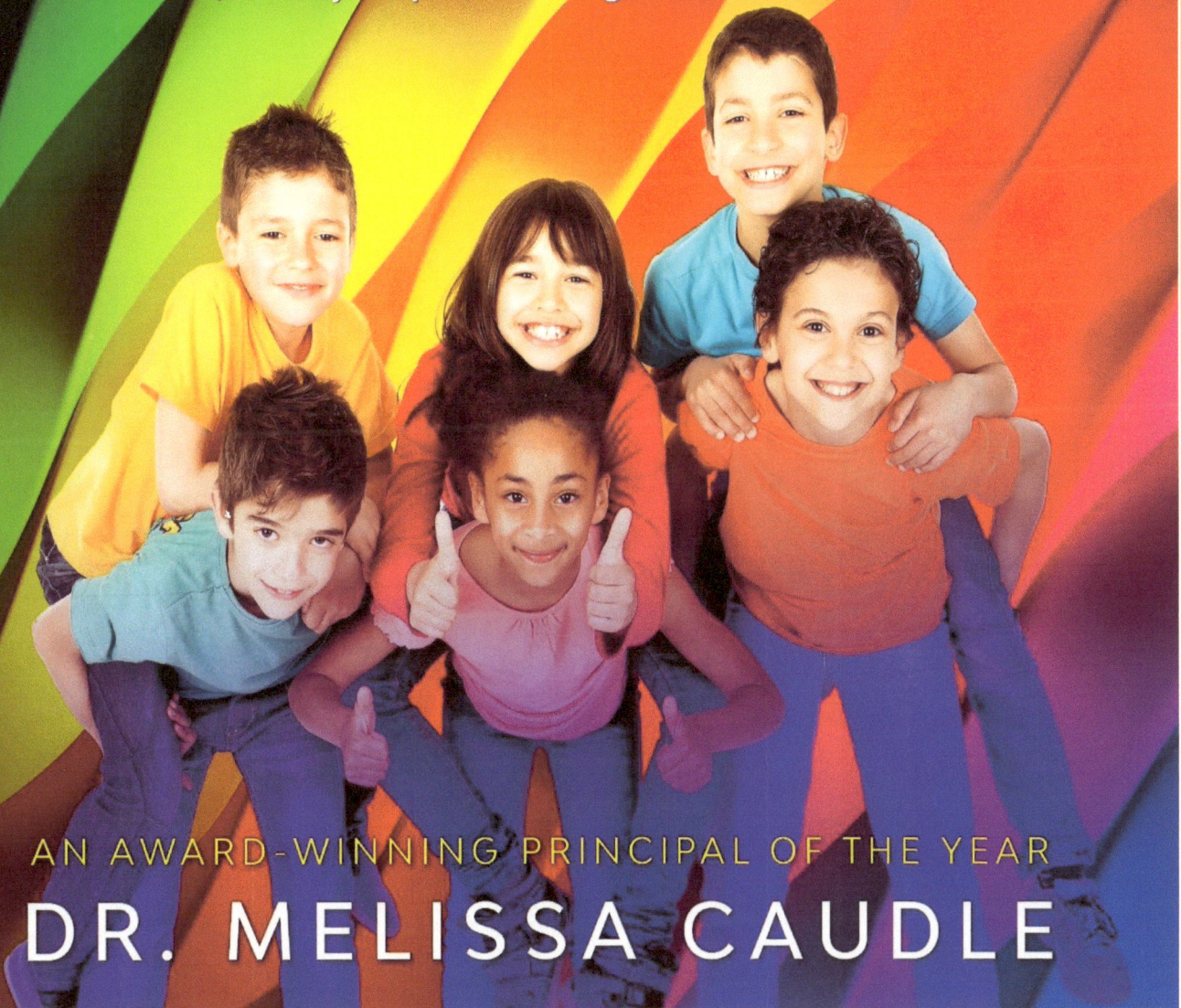

AN AWARD-WINNING PRINCIPAL OF THE YEAR

DR. MELISSA CAUDLE

The Creek Dweller
in the Bayou

Dr. Melissa Caudle

Illustrated by Endar Novianto

CERTIFICATE
of
COMPLETION

CONGRATULATIONS

PRESENTED TO

FOR

Learning to Write Numbers, Months and Names in Cursive

Blythe

_____
DATE

_____
SIGNATURE

UPPERCASE CURSIVE ALPHABET

Let's review how to write the uppercase alphabet. Trace over each uppercase letter until you are comfortable writing each one.

A B C D E F G H I J K L M N O P Q R S T U V W Y X Z

$$\mathcal{A} \quad \mathcal{B} \quad \mathcal{C} \quad \mathcal{D}$$

$$\mathcal{E} \quad \mathcal{F} \quad \mathcal{G} \quad \mathcal{H}$$

$$\mathcal{I} \quad \mathcal{J} \quad \mathcal{K} \quad \mathcal{L}$$

$$\mathcal{M} \quad \mathcal{N} \quad \mathcal{O} \quad \mathcal{P}$$

$$\mathcal{Q} \quad \mathcal{R} \quad \mathcal{S} \quad \mathcal{T}$$

$$\mathcal{U} \quad \mathcal{V} \quad \mathcal{W} \quad \mathcal{X}$$

$$\mathcal{Y} \quad \mathcal{Z}$$

Hello! My name is Blythe. It is great to see you again.

Are you ready to learn how to write numbers, colors, seasons, months, and names in cursive? For each exercise, follow the numbered arrows, and then trace over the dot-to-dot words followed with independent practice on the lines. Let's go!

Absolute Author
Publishing House

CHILDREN'S DIVISION

Cursive Writing Numbers, Colors, Seasons, Months, & Names
Copyright © 2020
Dr. Melissa Caudle

Publisher: Absolute Author Publishing House
Editor: Dr. Carol Michaels
Cover Designer: MD. Sheikh Shoeb Uddin
Illustrator: Sidra Ayyaz

ISBN: 978-1-951028-77-0

1. Education   2. English as a Second Language   3. Handwriting

Dear Parents and Teachers:

Welcome to Book 2 in this series "Having Fun Cursive Writing with Blythe." In Book 1, your child learned how to write the cursive alphabet. In this book, your child will master cursive writing by learning how to write numbers, seasons, months, and names. As a retired educator, mother, and grandmother, I know the importance of having fun for children as they learn. Shouldn't all learning? I'm glad you agree.

When my grandchildren informed me that schools no longer taught cursive handwriting, I was horrified. Learning to write cursive is an important skill and research as proven that children who do learn, it impacts their thinking, language, and memory. Repeated studies have proven the connection between the left and right hemispheres of the brain when writing. I have outlined this book strategically for your child to master cursive writing. Here is the order that your child will learn to write cursive in this book.

1. Numbers
2. Seasons
3. Months of the year
4. Colors
5. Names

I have carefully constructed this series of workbooks using sound principles of teaching. Think of this method as teaching your child to write the alphabet one letter at a time, only not in alphabetical order. Your child must practice and master writing the cursive alphabet in Book 1 before moving to the other books in the series. That is why you need to have Book 4, *Lined Cursive Writing Practice Book,* for additional practice.

This cursive handwriting book series is divided into four books.

- Book 1 – Tracing and Writing the Cursive Alphabet in Lower and Uppercase from A – Z
- **Book 2 – *Cursive Writing Numbers, Colors, Seasons, Months, & Names***
- Book 3 – *Writing Short Words and Sentences in Cursive*
- Book 4 - *Lined Cursive Writing Practice Book*

Please remember, writing in cursive is a fun activity, as well as your child learning a new skill.

Supplies Needed:

#2 Pencil

Eraser

Pencil Sharpener

*For added practice, consider purchasing the *Lined Cursive Writing Practice Book.*

TIPS FOR PARENTS

1. When working with your child, monitor their progress, and demonstrate how to trace the letters and then to write them. Children learn by watching.

2. Make sure there is sufficient light in the area.

3. Always use the lined cursive paper when teaching your child. It is challenging for them to use unlined paper or regular lined paper used in school. It is wise to invest in my Book 5 *Lined Cursive Writing Practice Book* to provide your child with plenty of space to practice writing in cursive.

4. Make sure that your child is sitting at a table or desk where they can comfortably write and have excellent posture. It is okay if your child wants to move their paper diagonally to create a slant for writing. It is the most natural way. For right-handed children, the paper should be parallel with the child's hand slanted left at about a twenty percent angle. If you have a left-handed child, they will slant their paper to the right. The essential factor is that they are comfortable.

5. With every exercise in this book, have your child trace over the guided arrows, see sample below, for each alphabet until they are comfortable before moving to the dot-to-dot letter, followed by independent practice on the lined page area.

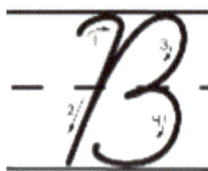

Happy cursive writing,

Dr. Melissa Caudle